ROBERT LOUIS STEVENSON
from a photograph by Lloyd Osbourne
taken in 1885 at Bournemouth

ROBERT LOUIS STEVENSON

By G. B. STERN

Gladys Bronwyn

PUBLISHED FOR

THE BRITISH COUNCIL
and the NATIONAL BOOK LEAGUE

BY LONGMANS, GREEN & CO., LONDON, NEW YORK, TORONTO

LONGMANS, GREEN & CO. LTD.
48 Grosvenor Street, London W.1
Thibault House, Thibault Square, Cape Town
605–611 Lonsdale Street, Melbourne, C.1.

LONGMANS, GREEN & CO. INC.
119 West 40th Street, New York 18

LONGMANS, GREEN & CO.
20 Cranfield Road, Toronto 16

ORIENT LONGMANS LTD.
Calcutta   Bombay   Madras
Delhi   Hydrabad   Dacca

First published in 1952
Reprinted, 1961

Printed in Great Britain by
F. Mildner & Sons, London, E.C.1

¶ ROBERT LOUIS STEVENSON was born in Edinburgh on 13 November 1850. He died on 3 December 1894 and was buried on Mount Vaea, Samoa.

ROBERT LOUIS STEVENSON

ROBERT LOUIS STEVENSON was born on 13 November 1850; therefore 1950 was his centenary year. His stepdaughter remembers a note he wrote his wife bidding her not delay too long with his biography after his death, for 'my fame will not last more than four years'. By this modest and perfectly sincere estimate, we can imagine how astonished he would have been, in 1935, at a set of Samoan stamps showing his grave on the crest of Mount Vaea, and his house, Vailima; and another rarer issue, in 1939, commemorating the twenty-fifth anniversary of the Australian landing on the island at the outbreak of the 1914–18 war, somewhat irrelevantly pictured with a head of Robert Louis Stevenson. Even more amazed would he have been by the centenary that in print and on the air honoured his name and proclaimed a longer life than even a hundred years for *Treasure Island*, *The Strange Case of Dr. Jekyll and Mr. Hyde* and the two brief verses of *Requiem*, if for no other of his writings. It is hardly possible now to open a newspaper or a magazine without seeing 'Jekyll and Hyde' quoted either as a caption or in illustration of some debatable point of modern schizophrenia. 'Home is the sailor, home from the sea' is quoted nearly as often; in fact, at moments it becomes quite a struggle not to quote it. And the films have given *Treasure Island* as vivid a resurrection as any nineteenth-century writer could have desired who unconsciously employed such an excellent film technique as Stevenson; he said himself that he visualized his novels in a series of small, bright, restless pictures; 'Thus with imagined wing our swift scene flies in motion . . .' says the Chorus in Shakespeare's *Henry V*. And *The Wrecker*, for instance, employing the speed, energy, and facility of the camera 'on location', might certainly have been originally planned in terms of celluloid.

The Wrecker, however, is not to be listed among his books

that have survived in equal popularity with *Treasure Island*
and *Jekyll and Hyde*. Survival and popularity, as we are all
aware, are capricious matters and play tricks that no one can
ever foresee. Without doubt, his finest work was poured
into the first few chapters of *Weir of Hermiston; Kidnapped;*
two-thirds of *The Master of Ballantrae;* a half-dozen of his
short stories; about three poems; a generous handful of
the letters he wrote spontaneously from all over the world
to his friends and family, and one immortal letter that he
sent to be published with the title *An Open Letter to the Rev.
Mr. Hyde in Defence of Father Damien.*

The London in which Stevenson pretended to have set the
drama of *Jekyll and Hyde*, had it been called Timbuctoo or
Athens, would even then have been clearly recognizable as
his native Edinburgh. G. K. Chesterton was probably the
first to stress the significance of this, noticing how strangely
R.L.S. always produced his most vital work under the
stimulus of banishment; strangely, because creative artists
are said to draw constant nourishment from the soil where
their roots are deeply planted, and to wilt in exile; yet if we
except *Treasure Island*, Stevenson was not dominated by an
urgent need to write stories of Scotland till he left it behind
him for good. And in comic proof that his nostalgia was
reversible, *Treasure Island*, aching for adventure in the fierce
tropical heat of the Pacific, was mostly written in the mists
and grey cold of Braemar. Certainly when he conceived
Kidnapped and *Jekyll and Hyde* in Bournemouth, his exile
from Scotland was not yet such an histrionic affair as it
would be in future years, when a sudden view from his high
snowy hut at Saranac was so poignantly to remind him of the
Solway shore, that straightway he began to write *The
Master of Ballantrae*, which was a masterpiece while he kept
the scene at Durrisdeer: the enemy brothers fighting their
duel by candlelight 'in a windless stricture of frost' pro-
vides one of those unforgettable scenes of literature which
have been far too often overlooked; to be classed with that
other tremendous fight in *Kidnapped*, when Alan Breck and

David Balfour defended themselves against a crew of fifteen in the round-house of the brig *Covenant*:

> The sword in his hand flashed like quicksilver into the huddle of our fleeing enemies . . . 'And O, man,' he cried in a kind of ecstasy, 'am I no a bonny fighter?'

The Master of Ballantrae can be read as a story of a dual personality less obviously confined in one body than Jekyll and Hyde. Two brothers stand for good and bad, love and hate. And in the course of time, hate wins. Henry, the gentle and the kind, is justified in hating James, incarnation of fascinating evil, if hate were ever justified. But James grows no less wicked while we have to watch Henry, a slave to his obsession, gradually drained of all good . . . till in the end, Henry and James are the same—and again Hyde has conquered Jekyll. Quiller-Couch was later to develop that sinister idea in a novel called *Foe-Farrell* which may well have been inspired by *The Master of Ballantrae*; for Q. was one of Stevenson's ardent disciples; he it was who exclaimed for all the band of younger writers, on hearing of the death of R.L.S.; 'Now there's no one left to write for!' And to him was entrusted the task of finishing Stevenson's *St. Ives*, the book which started with a breathtaking narrative of a French prisoner's escape from Edinburgh Castle.

Inspiration: the act of drawing air into the lungs. So says the dictionary. Thus a vivid memory of Edinburgh, its force and impact, its authentic speech, character, and flavour, was enough of inspiration for those magnificent scenes in *Weir of Hermiston*, between the stern old Justice-Clerk and his rebellious only son. It may truthfully be said of Stevenson that all his days were brave, but that in his early youth they were also days of bravado; and it had taken him more than twenty years to realize how his own father had suffered in the clash of opinions with a headstrong only son. In that one scene of *Weir*, Thomas Stevenson, engineer to the Commissioners of Northern Lights, stern Puritan

and deeply loving father, was at last triumphantly under-
stood. And in the same book, the pure moorland air up
by the Praying Weaver's Stone at Cauldstaneslap, where
Archie Weir and Christina Elliot discover and confess their
love, put an end to a notion that Stevenson could not write a
great love-scene. Indeed, his special genius may be described
as this useful power of identification with each of his
characters; *A Lodging for the Night*, where François Villon,
after assisting in a brutal tavern murder, stumbles in terrified
flight through the snow-covered street of medieval Paris,
does not merit our praise for its virtuosity alone, nor for
its strict economy of phrase and adjective, but because the
same man who at the end of his life could plunder the soul of
Adam Weir, here, fairly near the beginning of his career,
could also by inspiration—identification—what you will!—
enter fully into the motives, philosophy, and rationaliza-
tions of a fifteenth-century poet and scamp. And Villon's
sardonic reactions to normal good treatment, displayed in
argument with his courteous host, the Seigneur de Brisetout,
are as exciting as the pace and action of the earlier half of the
story. One can find many similar examples of Stevenson's
uncanny coalition with villany. All the people in *The
Ebb-Tide* are horrible—one does not so much read the last
few chapters as feel them crawling up one's spine; and
Long John Silver, James Durie of Ballantrae, or Jekyll's
schizophrenic double, Hyde, might really cause readers to
wonder whether he could present Brother Good without Sister Dull as an inevitable companion . . . till David
Balfour, Jim Hawkins, Kirstie and her enchanting niece
Christina join the procession of his living characters. Henry
James said of R.L.S.: 'He belongs to the class who
have both matter and manner, whom life carries swiftly
before it, and who communicate and signal as they go.'
He very rarely 'communicated' in poetry, and when he
did, wrote his verses literally like an amateur; that is to
say, like an impetuous fellow in love; not, as when he
wrote prose, with the severe self-discipline of a professional

unremittingly engaged in a life-and-death struggle with style. Which is probably why critics are rather apt to underrate the stature, or rather the depth, of an occasional poem embodying his creed:

> To thrill with the joy of girded men,
> To go on for ever and fail and go on again,
> And be mauled to the earth and arise,
> And contend for the shade of a word and a thing not seen with
>   the eyes:
> With the half of a broken hope for a pillow at night
> That somehow the right is the right
> And the smooth shall bloom from the rough:
> Lord, if that were enough?

To browse through any of the several uniform editions of Stevenson's works must bring the conclusion that there is nothing uniform about them except their bindings. As we race through the titles, it emerges clearly, however, that to dismiss him as the author of 'no more than a handful of stories for boys' is not only a fallacy, but a fallacy so preposterous that only Stevenson himself could be forgiven for such a statement, spoken once to Lloyd Osbourne in a mood of weariness shortly before his death. True that when he had grown to be a celebrity in a big way, a midshipman from H.M.S. *Curaçoa*, hospitably made free of the library at Vailima, suddenly exclaimed: 'Good Lord, I never realized! *He's* the josser who wrote *Treasure Island*.' True, also, that elderly men gulped down *Treasure Island*, unashamed to have become boys for a spell; though when it was reported to the author how Gladstone read it through in a night, he merely remarked coldly that Gladstone would have done better to have attended to the business of the Empire. For Stevenson was by nature a hero-worshipper, a passionate champion of lost causes, and could not forgive the Prime Minister responsible for Gordon's death on the steps of the Residency at Khartoum.

But setting aside *Treasure Island* and *Kidnapped*, nobody in their senses would benevolently produce *The Ebb-Tide* as suitable literature for juveniles; nor, with all its promising title, *The Wrecker;* nor the tale of what happened on the Beach of Falesà; nor *The Master of Ballantrae;* nor *Weir of Hermiston*, nor *Jekyll and Hyde*, nor *Father Damien*. In short, and after a brief biographical sequence of events and dates, one could draw up a fairly adequate survey of the Life and Works of Robert Louis Stevenson by investigating and if necessary clearing away every fallacy that during the last fifty-seven years has grown up to surround and obscure the truth.

But first the sequence.

His father, Thomas, was a son of Robert Stevenson, founder of the family of Lighthouse Engineers who built Skerryvore, Bell Rock, and other famous towers round the rocky coast of Scotland. His mother was Margaret, youngest daughter of the Rev. Lewis Balfour, Minister at Colinton. A French strain in the Balfours became evident in the appearance of R.L.S., and in his gaiety and resilience that conflicted with the Scottish strain of melancholy, integrity and forthrightness inherited from the Stevenson side. He was a delicate only child, adored by his parents and 'Cummy' his devoted nurse, a strongly religious woman with a dramatic vein, from whose fund of stories about the Covenanters he drew his passionate interest in that dour portion of his country's history. To her he dedicated *A Child's Garden of Verses:* '. . . From the sick child now well and old'—but the sick child was rarely to be well and never old. It is strange that the Stevensons remained so long in 8 Howard Place, the gloomy, sunless house where Louis was born; much mischief had been done by the time he was three and they moved on to Inverleith Terrace, and four years later to 17 Heriot Row. Thomas Stevenson had no rigid ideas about education; he was a delightful playmate, content that Louis's attendance at school should be irregular and undistinguished. Sometimes his mother took him abroad, for his health and hers; and often he stayed with a throng of cousins at Colinton Manse, holidays happily commemorated in *A Child's Garden of Verses*. Several of his essays, notably *Penny Plain and Twopence Coloured* and *The Lantern Bearers* would never have been written had he not played enthusiastically with a toy theatre, or joined other boy adventurers with evil-smelling lanterns strapped under their coats.

When Louis was seventeen, his father bought Swanston Cottage in the Pentland Hills near Edinburgh. Louis loved Swanston; loved his long rambles with his father or alone over the slopes of Allermuir, Caerketton, and Halkerside—his 'hills of home'. Thomas Stevenson took it for granted that presently he would enter the family profession; but Louis soon showed he was temperamentally and physically unsuited for superintending the construction of harbours and lighthouses on the bleak wind-swept coast of Fife; so he was allowed to go to Edinburgh University on condition that he studied Law, and left writing to be a sideline. The young man idled, loafed, took up with the wrong companions, and caused serious anxiety at home and grimly disapproving looks from the 'unco guid' citizens of Edinburgh, by his wayward, extravagant behaviour; he did eventually obtain his Law Degree, and, surprisingly, even a Silver Medal from the Royal Scottish Society of Arts for reading a paper on a New Form of Intermittent Light.

Violent quarrels with his father on conduct and religion led to their tragic estrangement; and seriously affected by the unhappiness and misunderstandings that surrounded him, Louis fell ill. He was sent for convalescence to some cousins in Suffolk. Here, in 1873, he met Mrs. Sitwell, who, until he married, was to be the strongest influence in his life. Mrs. Sitwell made him consult a lung specialist. 'Ordered South' was the verdict, and a stay of several months in the South of France, writing and slowly recuperating. But before he went, she introduced him to Sidney Colvin, and they encouraged young Stevenson to become a professional writer. Through Colvin's good offices, he succeeded in getting his first essay, *Roads*, published in *The Portfolio*, using the initials that were to become his signature tune: R.L.S.

Back again from the Riviera, some of his essays were accepted by the *Cornhill*; and he was taken by the editor, Leslie Stephens, to see another contributor, W. E. Henley, who was having treatment under Lister at the Edinburgh Infirmary. A memorable friendship sprang up; and when Henley was appointed to the editorship of *The London Magazine*, R.L.S. contributed *The New Arabian Nights*. This, however, did not immediately follow their first encounter; for in 1877, R.L.S. joined his cousin R. A. M. Stevenson (Bob) in a long careless sojourn with the artists' colony at Barbizon. From a canoe trip on an inland voyage through the canals, waterways, and rivers of Northern France, he gained material for his first book; and on his return to the Forest of Fontainebleau, he saw and fell in love with Fanny Osbourne, a beautiful married woman from Indiana, staying at the inn at Grez with her two children, Isobel and Lloyd. The next two years he spent his summers with her in France, his winters in Edinburgh, and established a growing reputation as a writer, mainly with essays on a variety of literary subjects. In 1878 Fanny Osbourne felt she had to return to her husband in California, and R.L.S. went on his lonely travels with a donkey in the Cevennes. (Modestine was chosen by several children in a centenary competition for an essay on Stevenson's most bewitching character!)

A year later, hearing that Fanny, ill and unhappy, was starting divorce proceedings, Stevenson wrenched himself from his home, his parents, and his potential career, and against the strong advice of all his friends (Henley's went beyond all reason), followed her to California. He chose to travel steerage to New York, and again fell dangerously ill from the further drastic experience of crossing the plains of America in the emigrant train. Twice he nearly died, first at Monterey and then in San Francisco, where he struggled through conditions of stark poverty to maintain himself by his writing without appealing for help from home. Finally, gaunt as a wolf and hardly able to stand, he married Fanny. The doctor told her he could not live more than a few months; she kept him alive and creative for fourteen years. After their honeymoon in the Californian mountains, where he wrote *The Silverado Squatters*, a longed-for reconciliation with his parents drew him back again to Scotland, bringing his wife and his stepson, Lloyd Osbourne. Mr. and Mrs. Thomas Stevenson soon became tenderly attached to Fanny; and she and Louis alternated between summers spent with them at Pitlochry and Braemar, and winters in Davos. On a rainy day in the Highlands, Stevenson began writing *Treasure Island* to amuse Lloyd—and himself. He finished it at Davos, 1882, and it ran as a serial in *Young Folks*, where it was oddly unsuccessful with its juvenile readers. His lungs could not stand the climate of Scotland, and three times thay had to go on these weary pilgrimages to the Swiss mountains; but in whatever state of bad health, except when he was nearly dying, he could not afford to let up on his writing. Besides finishing *Treasure Island* at Davos, he produced a first-class biography; the 'Memoir' of Fleeming Jenkin, tribute of gratitude to a dead friend, the University Professor who had had the perception to stand by him in 'the coiled perplexities of youth', during his wild Odyssey through the taverns and brothels of Edinburgh.

In 1882, he and Fanny moved to the South of France. Châlet la Solitude at Hyères was their first home together and he said of it, years afterwards, in a letter: 'I've only been happy once, at Hyères.' There he wrote *Prince Otto;* and exultantly put on record that he received a hundred guineas from Cassells for the publishing rights of *Treasure Island;* which seemed to him then a very large sum.

A dangerous haemorrhage brought him to the state of lying in a dark room, forbidden to speak, his arm strapped to his side; rendered incapable of sterner efforts as a wage-earner, he scribbled a great many letters, a lot of gay nonsense, and most of *A Child's Garden of Verses*. On receiving news that Thomas Stevenson was failing, they returned and settled down at Bournemouth in a house his father bought for Fanny, which Louis chose to call Skerryvore.

During most of their three years in Bournemouth, Stevenson was confined to his detested bed, an apparently incurable invalid. *Kidnapped* brought him an unsensational meed of fame; but there was the desparate nightmare of perpetually needing money which probably evoked the actual nightmare which was to find it. *The Strange Case of Dr. Jekyll and Mr. Hyde* leapt at once into amazingly big sales; it was pirated in America, where its popularity brought Stevenson his first experience, half astonished, half amused, as an idol of the public. For in 1887, after his father's death, he crossed the Atlantic on board the *Ludgate Hill*, with his mother, Fanny, Lloyd, and a merry cargo of apes and stallions.

In New York he soon had enough of adulation; his health collapsed once more, and he was banished to Saranac, the American equivalent of Davos, a small health resort high in the Adirondacks. Here was born *The Master of Ballantrae*, and, in collaboration with young Lloyd Osbourne, a gorgeous piece of buffoonery: *The Wrong Box*.

After a biting winter in the snows, his American publisher, Scribner's, commissioned a volume on the South Seas. Stevenson used his patrimony to charter a luxury yacht in San Francisco, and, still accompanied by his family, sailed on the *Casco* for the Marquesas, Tahiti, and the Sandwich Islands, a voyage that was a significant success from every point of view except the book itself; commissioned work never suited him, for the results were always laboured, overscrupulous, and disappointing, and he then had to cope with misgivings as to whether in honesty he should return the advances and cancel the contracts.

Once at sea, his health and activities were always miraculous to those who had hitherto only known him as an invalid on land. He struck up enduring friendships with native kings, dark warriors and princesses, traders and sailors and missionaries of all nations, and with a touching group of lepers, old men and children, whom he encountered on his visit to the island of Molokai. In 1889 he paid off the *Casco*, Mrs. Thomas Stevenson returned to Scotland, and he stayed on with Fanny and Lloyd for nearly six months at Honolulu, where he finished *The Master of Ballantrae* and *The Wrong Box*. Then he went on a further exploration of the more uncharted archipelago of the South Pacific, finally making harbour at Apia, on Opolu, one of the Samoan Islands—(the sequence of Robert Louis Stevenson's addresses are a horror to any conscientious biographer). They were so delighted with the climate and the beauty of the place that they bought an estate half-way up Mount Vaea, where he and Fanny proposed to build a house in which to spend their winters. It fell out, however, that another serious haemorrhage at Sydney, on their way home in 1890, caused him to be forbidden on pain of death ever to revisit Europe or any temperate zone; the Tropics were his only chance. So with what grace he could muster—and to accept misfortune with good grace was among his happier talents—he built Vailima; sent Lloyd back to Edinburgh and Bournemouth to collect their furniture; and joined by his mother and Fanny's daughter, Isobel Strong, with her little son Austin, settled in Samoa till his death. During this last fruitful period he wrote *Catriona*, *The Wrecker*, *The Ebb-Tide*, *Records of a Family of Engineers*, *St. Ives*, several poems and ballads, four striking South Sea tales to be published as *An Island Night's Entertainment*, and those immortal chapters of *Weir of Hermiston* published posthumously in 1895. His stepdaughter, Belle, to whom he dictated them, relates how instinctively he found the right word, the right sentence and the right incident, as though he had written it all before and only had to reel it off from memory.

At Vailima he lived as a sort of chieftain, visited by pilgrims and friends from all over the world. His native staff were devoted to him, and he had all the generous instincts of a Scottish clansman in his abundant hospitality towards his own kin, friends and strangers—'distance no object'. In the troubled politics and wars of Samoa, the weaker side as usual claimed his Quixotic support; and he could not bear to remain a mere spectator at the defeat and banishment of the rebel King Mataafa whom he knew to be 'the one man of governing capacity among the native chiefs, and whom, in the interest alike of whites and natives, he had desired to see the Powers not crush, but conciliate'.

It would be literally true to say that since 1888, Stevenson's friends and readers had lost sight of him; which must mean that a man is either forgotten or becomes a legend while he is still alive. The spate and vitality of his intimate letters made it impossible that he should be forgotten, and his situation contributed to a tuppence-coloured legend which he would have repudiated with real exasperation, for it was alien to his nature to assume importance. John Steinbeck relates an incident heard from an old woman who in her childhood had had an encounter with R.L.S. at Monterey. 'It's not bad fun', he remarked, after the little girl had cheated him over a sale of blueberries, 'it's not bad fun, to be made a fool of for ten cents!'

But the man was over-strained and over-worked, and his friends' project for an Edinburgh Edition failed to reassure him that he might now safely take a rest for a while. On 3 December 1894, he was struck down by a cerebral haemorrhage and died within two hours.

Certain men have provocative personalities: H. G. Wells once remarked a little sadly, 'I don't know how it is, but whenever (a famous contemporary's name) is mentioned, there's a respectful hush, but when it's mine, there's a dog-fight!' The remark would be as true of Stevenson as of Wells; mention his name, and still, where anything is known about him at all, the result will not be indifference or calm high hymns of praise, but a dog-fight; for his centenary revealed that far from being moribund, a casual reference to Robert Louis Stevenson will cause as much red blood to spurt as made the decks slippery on board the brig *Covenant*.

Jekyll and Hyde was his first huge selling success in England and America; he wrote it as a shilling shocker, and it became popular at once and ever after as a symbolic portrayal of the dual nature of man, with the moral inverted; not to impress us by the victory of good over evil, but to warn us of the strength and ultimate triumph of evil over good once sin is suffered to enter human habitation. Yet neither was Jekyll intended as a simple personification of good, but as good trying to keep up appearances, good wishing to maintain its prestige while it stealthily enjoys 'going to the bad'; the author obviously regarded him as a contemptible Quisling who failed to put up any resistance movement against the invader. He once remarked to Andrew Lang, with admirable brevity: 'I want to write about a fellow who was two fellows'; and in a letter discussing the interdependence of Jekyll and Hyde, he admitted to an old dingdong battle which perpetually preoccupies the disreputable human soul: 'the only thing I feel dreadful about is that damned old business of the war in the members.' It cannot be denied that he was inordinately fond of sermonizing—'I shall preach on my death-bed'—but it always found a more vivid medium in fiction, through narrative and character, than when he indulged himself with composing half-hour sermons for an imaginary pulpit.

It is well known how he originally dreamt 'this fine bogey tale' and finished it in three days of furious writing, and then burnt the draft and re-wrote it in another three days, referring to his wife's objection that he had left out the allegory. Long afterwards, R.L.S. alluded to the book, casually, as the worst thing he had ever done; he never harboured pretty illusions about his own work. Although rueful and ashamed that his own angel always seemed to put up such a poor show, he was no hypocritical weakling like

Jekyll; and whatever enemy he carried within him it utterly lacked the callous cruelty of Hyde.

'The legend goes' is a scornful phrase used with conviction by both sides in a battle; for nearly every biography will reveal a small but wilful partiality, an almost invisible pendulum-swing towards this pile of evidence or that: 'Codlin's the friend, not Short'. . . . And where the matter rests upon surmise, the subconscious has to choose between a discreet and somewhat irritating type of biographical soft-pedalling—'we need touch but lightly on'— or an inevitable swing-over to the brutal realism of the De-bunking School, who have found a peculiar satisfaction in stressing the early swashbuckling period of an author whom they considered had received more than his share of senti-mental idolatry. Stevenson's fellow Scot, J. M. Barrie, re-ferred to 'R.L.S., these familiar initials . . . the best beloved in recent literature'; and this has helped towards an odd notion that to think of Stevenson by his surname, not by his initials, made all the difference between a realistic approach or an attitude of whimsical tenderness—which seems to in-dicate that every biography of Shaw referring to him as G.B.S. must necessarily mean that we are dandling him in our arms! Probably Robert Louis Stevenson signed his earlier essays with his initials for the sake of convenience and brevity; he could hardly have known that after his death they would be condemned as a culpable form of petting-party. On the other hand, the pro-Stevenson brigade often damage their own cause by reproducing portraits of a pic-turesque invalid with untidy hair lapping his shoulders, and a smile of ineffable sweetness. (One of those it must have been that the little Samoan boy, Pola, threw on the floor when directly after Tusitala's death, he begged for his 'sun-shadow'. ' "I will not have that!" he cried. "It is pig-faced. It is not the shadow of our chief." He leaned against the door and wept.') That long hair of Stevenson's has become, so to speak, a King Charles's head to the scorn-ful; he may have started it in a period of youthful folly, from the desire to be unconventional; and later, while he lived in a northern climate, in perpetual danger of tuberculosis, his doctors would not allow him out for fear of cold; but every portrait extant from the South Seas during the four years before his death, shows the fallacy of still considering this fantastically thin man as an invalid: his hair was short, his clothes as normal as comfort and the tropical climate permitted; he spent hours every day in the saddle without fatigue, galloping over rough country; and days and weeks at sea on a tramp steamer, never noticing the lack of amenities in the questionable jollity of thrashing through typhoon and hurricane. Gardening in its herbaceous-border sense had never appealed to him at Bournemouth, but at Vailima this feeble dilettante hacked down trees and tore up masses of jungle growth before he even settled down to his morning's professional work. He laughed when threatened with expatriation by the furious German officials at Apia . . . but there was no laughter in his reaction to the news that Mataafa's warriors were being foully treated in prison. Everyone was afraid to interfere till Stevenson went storming down to the rescue in one of his crusading rages, bringing his men loaded with food, setting them to light the great ovens and clean out the stinking cells, attending to the victims who had been flogged through the streets, bringing the doctor to attend to them (and paying for it), and finally shaming the officials till they could no longer look the other way while these monstrous abuses were not only denounced but remedied by that troublesome writer who so maddeningly refused to mind his own business and remain writing nice books in his nice home half-way up a mountain.

For at all instances of cruelty or injustice to the oppressed, he flared up in a moment. From his childhood he had wanted to be a soldier; he loved fighting, but, he said, hated people to be angry with him—'the uncomfortable effect of fighting'—shrewdly laying his finger on the weak spot. And should one appear to dwell overlong on Stevenson's personality at the expense of concentrating on his work—or Works—it would only be a false detachment to allot him a final place in literature without an attempt to understand that what he was and why, must include so much of what he did and how. Writers like Byron or Burns, Shelley or Stevenson, are handicapped through the possession of a certain exciting quality in their make-up and the involuntary drama of their death. Neither was he at all the type conveyed in that nauseous phrase, 'a man with the heart of a boy'; his faults were essentially those of an adult male: a strong, hot temper with frequent use of strong, hot language; inconsiderate on a really grand scale (despite all his natural kindness) as regards the physical comfort of those around him, having himself no use for physical comfort; improvident in his generosity; wildly extravagant, and then given to moods of deep melancholy at the resulting state of his affairs.

When we encounter Henley's 'assassin' review in the *Pall Mall Magazine*, eight years after Stevenson's death, his lament for a lost friend whose genius had (apparently) been thwarted, hampered, enslaved, intimidated, deluded, badgered, and forced into mere wage-earning by the gloomy, respectable, material-minded woman with whom he had been press-ganged into marriage, we are up against another fallacy of such controversial proportions that it would take several volumes to go into the matter thoroughly and sift delusion from fact. Fanny Stevenson's place has often been in the dog-house; but Colvin left behind, for the guidance of 'all future biographers of R.L.S.' a round authoritative statement beginning:

> With reference to the causes of estrangement and in the actual quarrel, between Stevenson's widow and sometime old friend William Ernest Henley, it ought to be publicly known that the wife had ample and just cause for regarding the friendship as one that entailed risks to Louis's health and should be discouraged accordingly.

As we are most concerned with the indictment that his wife ruined his writing for the sake of material gain, let us point out that Stevenson certainly did write many promising essays before he married, and also *Travels With a Donkey*, *An Inland Voyage*, *The New Arabian Nights*, *The Amateur Emigrant*, and *Across the Plains*. But *after* he married Fanny Osbourne, besides the best of his short stories, he wrote *Treasure Island*, *Kidnapped*, *Catriona*, *Jekyll and Hyde*, *The Master of Ballantrae*, *Father Damien*, *The Ebb-Tide* and *Weir of Hermiston*; titles that speak for themselves. As for deploring her continual wary eye on the main chance, letters extant show that it was Colvin, not Fanny, who tried to hold him back from publishing *The Ebb-Tide*, a grim, squalid, powerful tale which might easily have spoilt his sales as a purveyor of juvenile fiction. And when Stevenson flamed out into his *Open Letter in Defence of Father Damien*, and read it to his family, gravely warning them that its publication might result in a libel action and the loss of all they had, she was the first to cry in a white heat of enthusiasm: 'Print it! Publish it!' In the dedication to *Weir of Hermiston*, he set down what may surely be taken for fair corroboration of his wife's influence:

Take thou the writing; thine it is. For who
Burnished the sword, blew on the drowsy coal,
Held still the target higher . . . who but thou?

Another absurd fallacy has been that he hated his father, whom nevertheless he speaks of in a letter as 'ever my dearest'; and in an essay of wonderful tenderness and perception, from *Memories and Portraits*, pays him a tribute of which any father might be proud. For undoubtedly R.L.S. honours the sound achievement of the 'Lighthouse Stevensons' far beyond his own as an author:

Say not of me that weakly I declined
The labours of my sires and fled the sea,
The towers we founded and the lamps we lit,
To play at home with paper like a child.

His summing-up of Lord Justice Weir—'steadfastly mounting the great bare staircase of his duty, uncheered and undepressed'—betrays again that no man could hope to win Stevenson by flamboyant exploits; he may have created Alan Breck for our delight, but we cannot suppose he thought him a character to emulate. Furthermore, in a letter to Henry James, he underlines his steady preference: 'The world must return some day to the word "duty", and be done with the word "reward". There are no rewards, and plenty duties.'

And that he was never, in the responsible sense of the phrase, the breadwinner and head of his own household is a fallacy so damaging to his good repute, that it should still be examined, contradicted, and once and for all thrown away. A hundred quotations from published letters, as well as from those not intended for publication, endorse his despair when illness tore gaps in his financial independence; and corroborate his passionate desire, at whatever expense of sweat and toil, to stand on his own feet and support a family without having to appeal for money to a wealthy father. Curious, that the swashbuckling author of *Treasure Island* should have been in essences 'a family man'; he liked having his family always around him—his mother, his wife, his two stepchildren, Lloyd and Belle, and Belle's little son Austin; liked to gather them under his roof-tree, declaring that they alone made exile bearable. His native staff looked up to Tusitala with more reverence as a father and a wise man than as a Teller of Tales; and as a father, he took trouble to make them see the ethics of why certain things may not be done: when any of them were caught out in wrongdoing, he held a formal court of justice to make sure of the full truth before inventing a mild punishment to fit the crime. The collection of Prayers he wrote, so often derided as merely fit for the nursery, were indeed deliberately written for the nursery; that is, for the clear understanding of those native converts to Christianity. This aspect of the White Man's Burden, combined with running a large estate, local politics, entertaining recklessly, and writing for a living, make it the more remarkable that he should have remained all his life so passionately pre-occupied with the campaign for upholding literary style.

There are those who often contemptuously dismiss Stevenson as 'a mere stylist'; as though a talent which was in the highest degree competent and fastidious, counted for no more than a prinking among words, stepping daintily along an imitation pergola, a sort of picot-edging to the silk. When he was young he scribbled that fatal phrase: 'I have played the sedulous ape'; Sir Max Beerbohm, with his nonchalant gift for hitting the nail on the head, supposed that this must be 'permanently kept in type in the journalistic offices . . . so frequently is it quoted against him'. Yet a neophyte who was later to develop into a magnificent stylist could ill afford *not* to play the sedulous ape; it meant no more than that he did not tumble into style as a child tumbles into water, but studied it more consciously and conscientiously than young writers usually do, by examining the technique of his great masters in craftsmanship. Speaking of himself as 'a working man', he assumed a title which he thoroughly deserved; he treated words courteously, not mangling them, though he confessed that his chief temptation was always 'to cut the flesh off the bones'. An old lady, Miss Adelaide Boodle, to whom he gave lessons in style when she was a girl and who was *persona grata* at their house in Bournemouth, wrote a delightful book about the Stevensons, where the very voice of R.L.S. can be heard teaching her how to write, and breaking her heart twenty times on every page: '*Never let a long sentence get out of hand*' he said to her. . . . Did he, by the way, ever think to say it to his friend, Henry James?

The friendship between Stevenson and Henry James, those unlikely bedfellows in literature, is brilliantly discussed in *A Record of Friendship and Criticism*, published in 1948 by Janet Adam Smith. Both these writers cared intensely about style, and believed in the future of literature as warriors go on believing in a cause that might sometimes look as though it were already lost. Stevenson's amusing piece of doggerel 'The Pirate and the Apothecary' might well stand for their prototypes; for it would be difficult to find a greater contrast than the Pirate in his characteristic mood of courage and laughing despair, and the Apothecary, meticulously weighing out his scruples and his sentences, tasting, measuring, conscientiously concerned as to their exact effect. This volume should rate high among the first half-dozen of a vast Stevenson bibliography; revealing how in their too rare conversation pieces as well as in their voluminous correspondence, both men recognized that a work of imagination must live by its own laws and only take so much from life as serves its purpose. Apothecaries do not, however, always dose themselves; and James's own style is a fairly potent reason why one would be more likely to choose G. K. Chesterton's estimate of R.L.S. as a stylist:

> The real defect of Stevenson as a writer, so far from being a sort of silken trifling and superficial or superfluous embroidery, was that he simplified so much that he lost some of the complexity of real life. He treated everything with an economy of detail and a suppression of irrelevance which had at last something about it stark and unnatural. He is to be commended among authors for sticking to the point; but real people do not stick quite so stubbornly to the point as that. . . . Though he may seem to describe his subject in detail, he describes it to be done with it; and he does not return to the subject. He never says anything needlessly; above all, he never says anything twice.

Nevertheless, and after all this, it must be admitted that, for some perplexing reason, Stevenson is not always *readable*; he demands an effort—no, fairer to say an initial effort; humour is not lacking, nor irony, nor the element of surprise, nor a plenitude of swift, exciting action; and the characters are sometimes disconcertingly alive—look at Alan Breck. The fault may be in our laziness to take trouble over an author already removed from contemporary interest, but not yet dead so long that we can surrender our reluctance to be rushed back from the present into the past.

But these strictures do not apply to his letters, which are undated in both senses of the word, and wholly delightful; excepting only a batch published separately as *Vailima Letters*, containing densely packed descriptions of his existence in Samoa, the scenery, climate, manners, customs, politics, flora and fauna of the place. Not having time to waste in writing of these twice over, he suggested to Sidney Colvin that they should be kept and docketed for publication after his death, and thus help provide for his family. But the hundreds of his other letters were intimate and spontaneous, not deliberately produced; they have been miscalled the letters of an egoist—again a fallacy; certainly they show a healthy—we underline the word—a *healthy* interest in himself and his mental processes, in his changes of heart as well as in his actual doings, but nothing to compare with their vital interest in his friends, displayed in a fury of questions as to their affairs and their work; delight in their successes, compassion for their sorrows, impatience if they dared withhold their personal news, indignation over wrongs done to them, eagerness to help at any cost to himself. Surely here is no record of egoism? And surely no egoist had friends as he had friends?

Friendship is a keepsake word, but it must form an essential feature of a writer's biography if we are to understand the different influences at different times of his life. Thus without his friend Henley, Stevenson might never have wasted his small reserve of nervous energy on writing plays; very bad, very rumbustious plays. Or he might have written better plays, for he was fundamentally a dramatist; all the most famous scenes of his novels and tales could be acted with hardly any change. Henley has contributed generously and far more than a small share towards Stevenson's growth as a writer, but little to the Stevenson biography except that one mysterious ill-judged attack in the *Pall Mall*, and one heart-broken poem: 'When we that were dear are all too near with the thick of the world between us. . . .' His nostalgic longing that one day they may 'lie in the peace of the Great Release as once in the grass together', quickens our glimpses of two young men idly a-sprawl on a slope of the Pentlands, talking and talking of the wonderful things they were to achieve. Yet still one cannot write a biography of either without feeling their war is not over. Final and visible causes for quarrel are always a little obscure; they begin many years before their protagonists are aware of it, and if we say heaven only knows when and where they end, it is in the hope that heaven at least does know. Kinder, meanwhile, to remember how Henley, after reading the posthumous fragment of *Weir of Hermiston*, wrote to Colvin a triumphant: 'I have found my Lewis again and in all his glory.'

On the whole, even in his profligate youth, Stevenson chose friends to match his strength, not his weakness; they make quite an impressive roll-call, headed by Colvin, Fleeming Jenkin, Henley, Will Low (the American artist), and Charles Baxter (writer to the Signet). Henry James and Edmund Gosse came later. The last published letter of Stevenson's—it may be the last he ever penned—was written to Gosse in deep affection and sadness:

> It is all very well to talk of renunciation, and of course it has to be done. But, for my part, give me a roaring toothache. . . . I have very little use for either watching or meditation. I was not born for age.

Henry James included in *Partial Portraits* a highly perceptive essay about Stevenson:

> He had incurred great charges, he sailed a ship loaded to the brim, so that the strain under which he sailed and wrought was immense; but the very grimness of it all is sunny, slangy, funny, familiar; there is a little of the effusive in his twinges of melancholy as of the priggish in his moments of moralizing. . . . He had a soundness all liberal and easy and born of the manly experience, that it is a luxury to touch.

A solemn young Scots writer called J. M. Barrie once hauled him over the coals for his want of proper seriousness, in a somewhat impertinent essay published in *An Edin-burgh Eleven:*

> . . . Mr. Stevenson has reached the critical point in his career, and one would like to see him back at Bournemouth, writing within high walls. We want that big book; we think he is capable of it, and so we cannot afford to let him drift into the seaweed.

Three years afterwards, R.L.S. wrote to him from Samoa in a spirit to serve as example to all famous writers of how to take with humorous good-nature the attacks of their lofty-minded juniors:

> . . . I have been off my work for some time, and re-read the *Edinburgh Eleven*, and had a great mind to write a parody and give you all your sauce back again, and see how you would like it yourself.

Another letter warmly praises *A Window in Thrums* ('There are two of us now who the Shirra might have patted on the head!—the Shirra was, of course, Sir Walter Scott, their hero') and ensured that Barrie, being human, became Stevenson's adoring, uncritical 'pen friend'; and we hear no more in his former lofty vein.

Andrew Lang, who frankly preferred the books to the man, wrote an introduction to the Swanston Edition, which should be read by the discriminate for its unbiased discrimination:

> Many circumstances caused Stevenson, when at his best, to be a historical novelist, and he is, since Scott and Thackeray, the best historical novelist whom we have. . . . Add to all this his notable eminence in tales of shorter scope; in essays, whether on life or literature, so various and original, so graceful and strong; add the fantasies of his fables, and remember that almost all he did is good. . . . With his faith, whatever its tenets may have been, was implicated his uneasily active conscience; his sense of duty. This appears to have directed his life; and was practically the same thing as his sense of honour. Honour, I conceive, is, in a phrase of Aristotle's, duty 'with a bloom on it'.

Sidney Colvin handed over his literary executor's privilege of writing the official *Life of Stevenson* to Graham Balfour, a cousin on the distaff side, who had stayed a year with Stevenson at Vailima. He did, however, himself edit the *Letters* with Notes and Introduction. J. A. Steuart's *Life of Stevenson*, without over-stressing those 'revelations' so dear to the Debunking School, has certainly freed itself from the affectionate partisan spirit of kinsman or personal friend. Rosalie Masson, too, has written a *Life* which is almost free from it; the Masson family knew him personally, for her father was a distinguished Professor at Edinburgh University at the same time as young Stevenson was cutting lectures and painting the town red. She wrote with authority and knowledge of her subject, rather than with intimacy; possibly she had not been allowed much intercourse with such a ne'er-do-well. She also edited a volume to which she gave the somewhat too sentimental title, *I Can Remember Robert Louis Stevenson*, containing nevertheless a variety of interesting matter that otherwise would have slipped through the grating and been swirled away; such as his comment, too wise not to be sad, to a servant eager to escape blame: 'Hush. . . . You know when one tries to justify oneself, one puts someone else in the wrong—and life is not possible under those conditions.'

For any student lost and bewildered by the multitude of Stevensoniana, a collection actually called *Stevensoniana*, by Sir John Hammerton, a notable beachcomber in the quest of contemporary material, ought not to be missed. But the 'sideline' biographies, with something of innocence—or shall we say naïveté—in their treatment, unprofessional and uncritical, with no literary 'approach', not out to 'refute' anything, nor swayed by post-mortem 'reasearch', these are often the most revealing provided they are written with integrity, free from the sweetness of marshmallow. In our selection, therefore, of the Hundred Best Books on Stevenson, we should include *A Chronicle of Friendship*, by Will Low, delightfully covering the Barbizon

and Grez period; and Lloyd Osbourne's Prefaces to the
Tusitala Edition; *This Life I've Loved*, by Isobel Field;
Mrs. Robert Louis Stevenson, by Nellie Sanchez (Fanny's
sister); *R.L.S. and His Sine Qua Non*, by Adelaide Boodle
(especially recommended), and *Memories of Vailima*, by both
his stepchildren.

The most distinguished contributions to Stevensoniana
produced by the Centenary Year were a localized study by
Moray McLaren on *Stevenson and Edinburgh*, a Preface by
John Hampden to *The Stevenson Companion*, felicitous title
to a summing-up that is often shrewd and always courteous
to the best companion in the world; and pre-eminently the
Collected Poems, edited by Janet Adam Smith, with an
Introduction and Notes.

But the thesis on Stevenson most deserving to be quoted
in full would cover 259 pages, every line brilliant and to the
point; so one can do no more than hope that G. K. Chesterton's biography, published in 1927, can still be obtained.
Chesterton's appreciation of Stevenson every now and then
might be comically inverted and read as Stevenson's appreciation of Chesterton, for they are extraordinarily similar in
their outlook and aims: 'Why should he be treated as a
liar', Chesterton asks, 'because he was not ashamed to be a
story-teller?'

A writer's centenary must inevitably lead to what is
rather pompously called an assessment of what the years
have tested for his survival value, which in Stevenson's case
has proved to be fairly robust. A motley collection could
be assembled from which I would select such seemingly
brittle testimonials of enduring usefulness as two roads,
two letters, and a page torn from a contemporary magazine.
Yet without undue sentimentality, one can hazard a guess
that these would have pleased him more than any Edinburgh Edition.

He had often said he wanted to be buried on top of
Mount Vaea, but no way existed through the impenetrable
tangle of scrub and undergrowth; so on the night of his

death, Lloyd Osbourne summoned the chieftains and told them Tusitala was dead, and what he had wished. With the first light of dawn, the stronger men set themselves to hew a track up the steep slope. By noon it was ready; and a long procession of mourners set out to climb the mountain road in the blazing heat, following the coffin carried shoulder-high on the spears of Samoan warriors.

The other road was opened only a couple of months before his death: until then, there had been no more than a path up to Vailima, branching off the main road which crossed the island. But when Mataafa's men were released from prison, they chose to remain behind, instead of returning straight to their homes and families, and replace the path by a connecting road sixty feet wide, themselves paying for all the necessary materials and maintenance while they built it. Then they set up a board with an inscription:

> Considering the great love of Tusitala in his loving care of us in our distress in the prison, we have therefore prepared a splendid gift. It shall never be muddy, it shall endure for ever, this road that we have dug.

Two roads. Two letters. Ori, sub-chief of the island of Tautira, had grown to love 'Rui' like a brother; and after Stevenson's departure in the *Casco*, he wrote:

> I make you to know my great affection . . . you looked from that ship, and I looked at you on the ship with great grief until you had raised the anchor and hoisted the sails. When the ship started, I ran along the beach to see you still. . . . I did not sleep that night, thinking continually of you, my very dear friend, until the morning. . . . Afterwards I looked into your rooms; they did not please me as they used to do. . . . I will not forget you in my memory. Here is the thought: I desire to meet you again. . . . It must be that your body and my body shall eat together at our table; there is what would make my heart content.

The second letter, a torn-off scrap written to Fanny in December 1894, needs no explanation:

> Dear Madam: Many thousands mourn the death of Robert Louis Stevenson, but none more than the blind leper of Molokai.

The final item for this random collection appeared fairly recently in a copy of *The Reader's Digest*. The author was telling of his unregenerate boyhood in Chillicothe, in the State of Missouri. The little town had no Public Library, so the boy and his gang read nothing but forbidden dime novels, shockers from the book-and-stationery shop:

> One day when I went into the shop to select a new Buffalo Bill, Mr. McIllwrath spoke to me in a lowered voice. 'You like to read exciting stories, don't you?' he said, and his eyes narrowed behind their smeared spectacles.
>
> 'Why, yes, sir', I said.
>
> 'All right, I'm going to tell you something I wouldn't tell just anybody. Back in the shop here, I've got the most exciting dime novel you ever read.' He led me to the rear of the shop. 'This book will cost you five times as much as a Buffalo Bill, but there's five times as much reading in it and it's about five times as exciting. Pirates, murder, hidden treasure—everything.'
>
> He took from a shelf a cheap red, cloth-bound book and slapped it affectionately. I read the title—*Treasure Island*.

The rest is quickly told; the whole of the gang came under the spell of Long John Silver and Jim Hawkins; they were converted, they learnt to read. But they kept *Treasure Island* hidden from the adults, quaintly assuming that any exciting story would be considered bad:

> '. . . Don't let your mother or sisters catch you with it. They might look inside and then there'd be a big stink and Mr. McIllwrath would get into trouble.'
>
> . . . It was with astonishment that I learned some years later that *Treasure Island* actually was a respectable book which could be read openly, and that some even regarded it as a classic.
>
> Mr. McIllwrath later sold us *Kidnapped*. . . . I suspect that the sour-faced old man was deliberately trying to develop a taste for literature in us.

There must be hundreds of Old Chillicothians and their like who could contribute similar experiences. Perhaps, after all, he sometimes wrote books for boys.

If any of these gestures were merely bogus, acts of nothingness which viewed from here and now would seem impotent as a wireless playing in an empty room, then one would have no reply to those of Stevenson's critics who maintain that he was little more than a pseudo-romantic. But on the contrary, they are in a true romantic tradition we have met before, of unselfconscious service to the human race (memory may set up the names of Chinese Gordon and Lawrence of Arabia); a tradition that appears to be founded on solid sense. Providing the right nourishment for a boy's mind makes sense; and to inspire a road to materialize where no road was before. And on the opening of the Road of Gratitude in 1894, Stevenson's Address to the Chiefs can surely be read and re-read for its contemporary message that begins with an echo from Ecclesiastes:

> There is a time to fight and a time to dig. You Samoans may fight, you may conquer twenty times, and thirty times, and all will be in vain. There is but one way to defend Samoa. Hear it before it is too late. It is to make roads, and gardens, and care for your trees, and sell their produce wisely, and, in one word, to occupy and use your country. If you do not, others will.
>
> . . . Because all things in a country hang together like the links of the anchor cable, one by another: but the anchor itself is industry.

Probably in another hundred years, if the conduct of the world has not changed beyond recognition, it may still be as relevant.

ROBERT LOUIS STEVENSON

A
Select Bibliography

(Place of Publication London, unless stated otherwise.)

Bibliographies:

BIBLIOGRAPHY OF THE WORKS OF ROBERT LOUIS STEVENSON, by W. F. Prideaux (1903; new edition, revised, edited, and supplemented by Mrs. L. S. Livingston, 1917)

—the revised edition is a standard work. Only the specialist in Stevensonian bibliography will need to consult, in addition, the important catalogues of the Widener and Beinecke Collections (see below).

CATALOGUE OF THE BOOKS AND MANUSCRIPTS OF ROBERT LOUIS STEVENSON IN THE LIBRARY OF THE LATE H. E. WIDENER. With a Memoir by A. S. W. Rosenbach. Philadelphia (1913)

—the Widener Collection is part of the Harvard College Library.

CATALOGUE OF A COLLECTION OF WRITINGS BY AND ABOUT ROBERT LOUIS STEVENSON, formed by E. J. Beinecke. Vol. I. Printed Books, Pamphlets, Broadsides, etc. Compiled by G. L. McKay. New Haven (1950)

—the first of two exemplary volumes of a catalogue, describing in detail the comprehensive collection of Stevenson's writings and Stevensoniana presented to Yale University on its 250th anniversary. Indispensable for the specialist.

Collected Editions:

EDINBURGH EDITION, edited by S. Colvin. 28 vols. (1894–8)

—the first collected edition.

A STEVENSON MEDLEY, edited by S. Colvin (1899).

THISTLE EDITION. 26 vols. New York (1902)

—issued to subscribers only.

ESSAYS AND CRITICISMS. Boston, Mass. (1903).

TALES AND FANTASIES (1905).

ESSAYS OF TRAVEL (1905).

ESSAYS IN THE ART OF WRITING (1905).

PENTLAND EDITION. With Bibliographical Notes by E. Gosse. 20 vols. (1906–7)

—Gosse's biographical and bibliographical notes were issued separately in a privately printed edition in 1908.

SWANSTON EDITION. With an Introduction by A. Lang. 25 vols. (1911–12).

POEMS AND BALLADS. Complete Edition. New York (1913).

COMPLETE POEMS. New York (1923)
—includes reprints of the three specious collections of poems privately printed for members of The Bibliophile Society, Boston, Mass. (2 vols., 1916; 1 vol. 1923). For an account of the fate of Stevenson's poetical MSS. after his death, see Introduction to *Collected Poems* (1950).

VAILIMA EDITION. Edited by Lloyd Osbourne, with Prefatory Notes by F. van de Grift Stevenson, and Portraits. 26 vols. New York (1921–3); London (1922–3).
Edited by Stevenson's wife and stepson. Limited edition of 2,000 copies.

TUSITALA EDITION. 35 vols. (1923–4)
—the best and most complete edition, fully annotated.

SKERRYVORE EDITION. 30 vols. (1924–6).

LOTHIAN EDITION. 21 vols. (1926–7).

COLLECTED POEMS. Edited, with an Introduction and Notes, by J. Adam Smith (1950)
—the definitive edition, with valuable notes.

THE STEVENSON COMPANION. Edited with an Introduction by J. Hampden (1950)
—contains *Weir of Hermiston* and a large selection of Stevenson's work.

R.L.S. An omnibus. Selected and edited by G. B. Stern (1950).

SELECTED POEMS, edited by G. B. Stern (1950).

TALES AND ESSAYS, edited by G. B. Stern (1950).

Separate Works:

THE PENTLAND RISING. A Page of History, 1666. Edinburgh (1866). *Essay.*

A NEW FORM OF INTERMITTENT LIGHT FOR LIGHTHOUSES. Edinburgh (1871). *Essay.*

ON THE THERMAL INFLUENCE OF FORESTS. Edinburgh (1873). *Essay.*

AN APPEAL TO THE CLERGY OF THE CHURCH OF SCOTLAND (1875). *Essay.*

AN INLAND VOYAGE (1878). *Travel.*

EDINBURGH. Picturesque Notes (1879). *Essays.*

TRAVELS WITH A DONKEY IN THE CEVENNES (1879). *Travel.*

VIRGINIBUS PUERISQUE AND OTHER PAPERS (1881). *Essays.*
Twelve essays reprinted, with one exception, from magazines.

FAMILIAR STUDIES OF MEN AND BOOKS (1882). *Essays.*
Nine essays reprinted from magazines.

NEW ARABIAN NIGHTS. 2 vols. (1882). *Fictions.*
Contains: Vol. I, 'The Suicide Club'; 'The Rajah's Diamond'.
Vol. II, 'The Pavilion on the Links'; 'A Lodging for the Night';
'The Sire de Malétroit's Door'; 'Providence and the Guitar'. All
these stories had previously appeared in magazines.

THE SILVERADO SQUATTERS. Sketches from a California Mountain
(1883). *Travel*
—originally published in the *Century Magazine*, 1883.

TREASURE ISLAND (1883). *Fiction*
—originally published as by 'Captain George North', in *Young Folks.*

PRINCE OTTO. A Romance (1885). *Fiction*
—originally published in *Longman's Magazine.*

A CHILD'S GARDEN OF VERSES (1885). *Verse*
—more than half of the text had previously appeared in a trial edition
with the title 'Penny Whistles'.

MORE NEW ARABIAN NIGHTS: THE DYNAMITER [In collaboration with
F. van de Grift Stevenson] (1885). *Fiction.*
Stevenson's wife was the sole author of *The Destroying Angel* and
The Fair Cuban.

THE STRANGE CASE OF DR. JEKYLL AND MR. HYDE (1886). *Fiction.*

KIDNAPPED: Being the Memoirs of the Adventures of David Balfour
in the year 1751 &c. (1886). *Fiction*
—originally published in *Young Folks.*

THE MERRY MEN and Other Tales and Fables (1887). *Fiction.*
Contains: 'The Merry Men'; 'Will O' the Mill'; 'Markheim';
'Thrawn Janet'; 'Olalla'; 'The Treasure of Franchard'. All these
stories had previously appeared in magazines.

THOMAS STEVENSON, CIVIL ENGINEER. (Priv. ptd. 1887). *Essay*
—also printed in the *Contemporary Review*, June 1887.

MEMOIR in *Papers Literary and Scientific by the Late Fleeming Jenkin*, edited by S. Colvin. 2 vols. New York (1887); London (1888). *Essay*
—Stevenson's 'Memoir' was published separately in New York, 1887.

MEMORIES AND PORTRAITS (1887). *Essays.*
Sixteen essays, mostly reprinted from magazines, and including 'Thomas Stevenson, Civil Engineer' (priv. ptd. 1887) and the 'Memoir' from *The Papers of H. Fleeming Jenkin*, 2 vols. (1887).

UNDERWOODS (1887). *Verse.*
Contains poems in English and Scots.

TICONDEROGA: A Poem. Edinburgh (priv. ptd. 1887). *Verse*
—originally published in *Scribner's Magazine*. rptd. in *Ballads* (1890).

THE BLACK ARROW: A Tale of the Two Roses (1888). *Fiction*
—originally published, as by 'Captain George North', in *Young Folks.*

THE MISADVENTURES OF JOHN NICHOLSON. A Christmas Story. New York (1888). *Fiction*
—piratically reprinted from *Cassell's Christmas Annual*, 1887.

THE MASTER OF BALLANTRAE. A Winter's Tale (1889). *Fiction*
—originally published in *Scribner's Magazine.*

THE WRONG BOX. [In collaboration with Lloyd Osbourne] (1889). *Fiction.*

FATHER DAMIEN: An Open Letter to the Rev. Dr. Hyde of Honolulu. London (1890). *Essay*
—originally published in the *Scots Observer*, May 1890, and privately printed in the same year in Sidney and Edinburgh.

BALLADS (1890). *Verse.*
Contains: 'The Song of Rabero'; 'The Feast of Famine'; 'Ticonderoga'; 'Heather Ale'; 'Christmas at Sea'.

ACROSS THE PLAINS, with Other Memories and Essays (1892). *Essays*
—twelve essays reprinted from magazines.

THE WRECKER. [In collaboration with Lloyd Osbourne] (1892). *Fiction*
—originally published in *Scribner's Magazine.*

A FOOTNOTE TO HISTORY: Eight Years of Trouble in Samoa (1892). *Essay.*

WAR IN SAMOA (priv. ptd. 1893). *Essay*
—originally published in the *Pall Mall Gazette.*

ISLAND NIGHT'S ENTERTAINMENTS (1893). *Fiction.*
Contains: 'The Beach of Falesà'; 'The Bottle Imp'; 'The Isle of Voices'. Preceded by publication in periodicals, 1891–2, and by a privately printed edition.

CATRIONA. A sequel to *Kidnapped*, being the Memoirs of the Further Adventures of David Balfour at Home and Abroad, &c. (1893). *Fiction*
—originally published as 'David Balfour' in *Atlanta.*

THE EBB-TIDE. A Trio and Quartette [In collaboration with Lloyd Osbourne] (1894). *Fiction*
—originally published in *To-Day.*

THE BODY SNATCHER. New York (1895). *Fiction*
—originally published in *Pall Mall*, Christmas number (1894).

THE AMATEUR EMIGRANT. From the Clyde to Sandy Hook. Chicago (1895). *Travel*
—originally published in Vol. III of the Edinburgh Edition of Stevenson's Works.

FOUR PLAYS [In collaboration with W. E. Henley] (1896). *Drama.*
Contains: *Deacon Brodie; Beau Austin; Admiral Guinea; Robert Macaire.* Each play was originally issued separately in a small privately printed edition, in 1880, 1884, 1884, 1885, respectively. The first three were published together as THREE PLAYS (1892).

THE STRANGE CASE OF DR. JEKYLL AND MR. HYDE, WITH OTHER FABLES (1896)
—the *Fables* were originally published in *Longman's Magazine.*

WEIR OF HERMISTON. An Unfinished Romance (1896). *Fiction*
—originally published in *Cosmopolis.*

A MOUNTAIN TOWN IN FRANCE. A Fragment. New York (1896). *Essay.*

SONGS OF TRAVEL and Other Verses (1896). *Verse*
—originally published in Vol. XIV of the Edinburgh Edition of Stevenson's Works.

ST. IVES. Being the Adventures of a French Prisoner in England [Completed by A. T. Quiller-Couch.] New York (1897); London (1898). *Fiction*

—the first thirty chapters, by Stevenson, were originally published in the *Pall Mall Magazine*.

PRAYERS WRITTEN AT VAILIMA. With an Introduction by Mrs. Stevenson. New York (1904); London (1905)

—originally published in Vol. XXI of the Edinburgh Edition of Stevenson's Works.

LAY MORALS AND OTHER PAPERS (1911). *Essays*

—ten essays originally published in magazines.

MEMOIRS OF HIMSELF. Printed from the Original Manuscript in the possession of H. E. Widener. Philadelphia (priv. ptd. 1912). *Biography.*

RECORDS OF A FAMILY OF ENGINEERS (1912). *Essays.*

THE HANGING JUDGE. A Drama in Three Acts and Six Tableaux. [In collaboration with F. van de Grift Stevenson.] With an Introduction by E. Gosse (priv. ptd. 1914). *Drama.*

THE WAIF WOMAN (1916). *Fiction*

—originally published in *Scribner's Magazine.*

ON THE CHOICE OF A PROFESSION (1916). *Essay*

—originally published in *Scribner's Magazine.*

NEW POEMS AND VARIANT READINGS (1918)

—an unedited reprint of the two carelessly compiled volumes issued in 1916 to members of The Bibliophile Society, Boston, Mass. For a severe but justified stricture on this compilation and its sequel see Introduction to *Collected Poems*, 1950.

THE MANUSCRIPTS OF ROBERT LOUIS STEVENSON'S *Records of a Family of Engineers*. The Unfinished Chapters. Edited, with an Introduction, by J. C. Bay. Chicago (1930).

> *Note:* The above list does not include many of the authorized privately printed editions, in which some of Stevenson's stories, essays, and poems first fippeared, among them the pamphlets printed on a hand-press at Davos, 1881–2, by Lloyd Osbourne, then a schoolboy; or a number of 'manufactured rarities' for the collectors' market, consisting of small, privately printed editions of occasional pieces of verse and prose from private collections in the U.S.A.

Letters:

VAILIMA LETTERS. Being Correspondence addressed by Robert Louis
Stevenson to Sidney Colvin, November 1890–October 1894 (1895).

IN THE SOUTH SEAS. New York (1896); London (1900)
—being an account of experiences and observations in the Marquesas,
Paumotus, and Gilbert Islands, in the course of two cruises, on the
yacht *Casco,* 1888 and the schooner *Equator,* 1889. Originally
published in the *New York Sun,* 1891, and privately printed in part
in *The South Seas* (1890).

LETTERS TO HIS FAMILY AND FRIENDS. Selected and Edited, with an
Introduction and Notes, by S. Colvin. 2 vols. (1899; new edition,
rearranged in 4 vols., with 150 new letters, 1911).

SOME LETTERS. Edited by Lloyd Osbourne (1914).

AUTOGRAPH LETTERS, ORIGINAL MSS., BOOKS, PORTRAITS, AND CURIOS
FROM THE LIBRARY OF THE LATE R. L. STEVENSON. 3 vols. New York
(1914–16)
—the catalogue of the sale at the Anderson Galleries, by Isabel Strong,
of her stepfather's literary property. One of the consequences of
this sale was the unauthorized and ill-considered production of the
'manufactured rarities' referred to in the Note at the foot of p. 40.

[Letters in] HENRY JAMES AND ROBERT LOUIS STEVENSON. A Record of
Friendship and Criticism. Edited, with an Introduction, by J. Adam
Smith (1948).

Some Biographical and Critical Studies:

ROBERT LOUIS STEVENSON, by W. Raleigh (1895)
—a lecture given at the Royal Institution, 1895, with additions.

IN STEVENSON'S SAMOA, by M. Fraser (1895),

THE HOME AND EARLY HAUNTS OF ROBERT LOUIS STEVENSON, by M.
Armour. Edinburgh (1895).

THE HOME LIFE OF ROBERT LOUIS STEVENSON, by J. Geddie (1898).

ROBERT LOUIS STEVENSON'S EDINBURGH DAYS, by E. B. Simpson (1898).

ROBERT LOUIS STEVENSON, by M. M. Black. Edinburgh (1898).
Famous Scots Series.

ROBERT LOUIS STEVENSON, by L. C. Cornford. Edinburgh (1899)
—modern English Writers Series.

ROBERT LOUIS STEVENSON: A Life Study in Criticism, by H. B. Baildon (1901).

THE LIFE OF ROBERT LOUIS STEVENSON, by Sir G. Balfour. 2 vols. (1901).

MEMORIES OF VAILIMA, by I. Strong and Lloyd Osbourne. New York (1902); London (1903)
—by Stevenson's stepchildren.

ROBERT LOUIS STEVENSON, by W. R. Nicoll and G. K. Chesterton (1902)
—little Books for Bookmen Series.

STEVENSONIANA, edited by J. A. Hammerton (1903); new and revised edition, Edinburgh (1907)
—uniform with the Pentland Edition of Stevenson's Works.

ROBERT LOUIS STEVENSON. An Essay, by Sir L. Stephen (1903).

ROBERT LOUIS STEVENSON: The Dramatist, by Sir A. W. Pinero (1903).

STEVENSON'S SHRINE. A Record of a Pilgrimage. By L. Stubbs (1903).

ROBERT LOUIS STEVENSON: A Record, an Estimate, and a Memorial—with hitherto Unpublished Letters from R. L. Stevenson in facsimile, by A. H. Japp (1905).

RECOLLECTIONS OF ROBERT LOUIS STEVENSON IN THE PACIFIC, by A. Johnstone (1905).

ROBERT LOUIS STEVENSON, by E. B. Simpson (1906).

WITH STEVENSON IN SAMOA, by H. J. Moors. Boston, Mass. (1910); London (1911).

ROBERT LOUIS STEVENSON IN CALIFORNIA, by K. D. Osbourne. Chicago (1911).

ROBERT LOUIS STEVENSON, by I. Strong (1911)
—Little Books on Great Writers Series.

THE R.L.S. ORIGINALS, by E. B. Simpson (1912).

A CHRONICLE OF FRIENDSHIPS, 1873–1900, by W. H. Low (1908)
—with illustrations by the author.
R.L.S. AND HENRY DRUMMOND, by A. Webster (1912).

ROBERT LOUIS STEVENSON. The Man and his Work (1913)
—an extra number of *The Bookman*. Includes reproductions of many portraits.

R.L.S., by F. Watt (1913).

ROBERT LOUIS STEVENSON, by R. O. Masson (1914; revised edition 1920).

R. L. STEVENSON: A Critical Study by F. Swinnerton, (1914; new edition 1924).

ROBERT LOUIS STEVENSON AS A DRAMATIST, by Sir A. W. Pinero. New York (1914)
—a Lecture, edited by C. Hamilton.

IN THE TRAIL OF STEVENSON, by H. Clayton (1916).

A LAST MEMORY OF ROBERT LOUIS STEVENSON, by C. Eaton. New York (1916).

THE PENNY PIPER OF SARANAC: An Episode in Stevenson's Life, by S. Chalmers. Boston, Mass., and New York (1916).

A BOOK OF R.L.S. Works, Travels, Friends, and Commentators, by E. Brown (1919).

ROBERT LOUIS STEVENSON. Some Personal Recollections, by C. J. Guthrie (Lord Guthrie). Edinburgh (1920).

ROBERT LOUIS STEVENSON: An Appreciation, by H. H. Harper. Boston (1920).

THE LIFE OF MRS. ROBERT LOUIS STEVENSON, by N. van de G. Sanchea (1920).

STEVENSON AT MANASQUAN, by C. Eaton. Chicago (1921)
—with a note on the fate of the yacht *Casco* by F. Dickie, and six portraits from Stevenson (in verse) by G. S. Seymour.

STEVENSON'S BABY BOOK: Being the Record of the Sayings and Doings of Robert Louis Balfour Stevenson, by M. Balfour [afterwards Stevenson], edited by K. D. Osbourne. San Francisco (1922).

I CAN REMEMBER ROBERT LOUIS STEVENSON, edited by R. O. Masson (1922; enlarged edition 1925)
—approximately one hundred short articles by as many contributors.

THE LIFE OF ROBERT LOUIS STEVENSON, by R. O. Masson. Edinburgh (1923).

ROBERT LOUIS STEVENSON AND FRANCE, by C. Sarolea. Edinburgh (1923).

AN INTIMATE PORTRAIT OF R.L.S., by Lloyd Osbourne. New York (1924).

ROBERT LOUIS STEVENSON: His Work and His Personality, edited by A. St. John Adcock (1924).
Essays by A. St. John Adcock; H. C. Beeching; Sir S. Colvin; S. R. Crockett; A. Gordon; E. Gosse; J. A. Hammerton; C. Lowe; I. MacLaren; N. Munro; Sir W. Robertson Nicoll; A. Noyes; Lloyd Osbourne; E. B. Simpson; Y. Y. (R. Lynd).

ROBERT LOUIS STEVENSON: Man and Writer. A Critical Biography, by J. A. Steuart (2 vols., 1924; I vol. 1926).

THE TRUE STEVENSON. A Study in Clarification, by G. Hellman. Boston, Mass. (1925)
—with portraits and facsimiles.

R.L.S. AND HIS SINE QUA NON [*i.e.*, Stevenson and his wife]. Flashlights from Skerryvore, by A. A. Boodle (1926).

CUMMY'S DIARY. A Diary kept by R. L. Stevenson's Nurse, Alison Cunningham, while travelling with him on the Continent during 1863. With a Preface and Notes by R. T. Skinner (1926).

R. L. STEVENSON AND THE BRIDGE OF ALLAN, with Other Stevenson Essays, by J. A. MacCulloch (1927).

ROBERT LOUIS STEVENSON, by G. K. Chesterton (1927).

ROBERT LOUIS STEVENSON AND THE SCOTTISH HIGHLANDERS. By D. B. Morris. Stirling (1929).

R. L. STEVENSON. A Study in French Influence, by H. D. MacPherson. New York (1930).

LA VOCATION DE ROBERT-LOUIS STEVENSON. Etude de Psychologie littéraire, par L. E. Chrétien. Paris (1930).

ROBERT LOUIS STEVENSON, by S. Dark (1931).

UN AMI DE FRANCE. R. L. STEVENSON DANS LE VELAY. Etude, suivie des Lettres écrites du Monastier en 1878, par F. Fabre. Clermont-Ferrand (1932).

ROBERT LOUIS STEVENSON AT DAVOS, by W. G. Lockett (1934).

ADRIFT IN THE SOUTH SEAS. Including Adventures with R. L. Stevenson, by T. M. MacCallum. Los Angeles (1934).

LA FRANCE DANS L'OEUVRE DE R. L. STEVENSON, par C. MacLean. Paris (1936).

ROBERT LOUIS STEVENSON, by J. Adam Smith (1937).

THIS LIFE I'VE LOVED, by Isobel Field (1937).

PRSBYTERIAN PIRATE. A Portrait of Stevenson, by D. N. Dalglish (1937).

ROBERT LOUIS STEVENSON, by S. Gwynn (1939)
—English Men of Letters Series.

STEVENSON AT SILVERADO, by R. Issler. Caldwell, Idaho (1939).

ROBERT LOUIS STEVENSON: An Englishman's re-study, after fifty years, of R.L.S. the Man, by H. J. Cowell (1945).

ROBERT LOUIS STEVENSON, by L. U. Cooper (1947).

ROBERT LOUIS STEVENSON, by D. Daiches. Glasgow (1947).

[THE POETRY OF R.L.S., by H. W. Garrod—in Essays presented to Sir Humphrey Milford (1948).]

ROBERT LOUIS STEVENSON, by J. Bowman (1949).

THE STRANGE CASE OF ROBERT LOUIS STEVENSON, by M. Elwin (1950).

ON THE BAT'S BACK. The Story of Robert Louis Stevenson, by M. S. Lawson (1950).

STEVENSON AND EDINBURGH. A Centenary Study, by M. MacLaren (1950).

VOYAGE TO WINDWARD: the Life of Robert Louis Stevenson, by J. C. Furnas (1952)
—contains interesting and authoritative matter only recently discovered; and setting forth in clear dispassionate style which carries conviction, a point of view defending Mrs. R. L. Stevenson, in considered opposition to her detractors.

INDEX TO PROSE

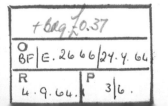